POPEYE GOES ON A PICNIC

POPEYE GOES ON A PICNIC

Story by CROSBY NEWELL
Pictures by BUD SAGENDORF

Wonder® Books
PRICE/STERN/SLOAN
Publishers, Inc., Los Angeles
1987

Copyright © 1958, 1986 by King Features Syndicate, Inc.
Published by Price/Stern/Sloan Publishers, Inc.
360 North La Cienega Boulevard, Los Angeles, California 90048

Printed in the United States of America. All rights reserved. No part of this publication may be reproduced, stored in a retrieval system, or transmitted, in any form or by any means, electronic, mechanical, photocopying, recording, or otherwise, without the prior written permission of the publishers.

ISBN: 0-8431-4131-X

Wonder® Books is a trademark of Price/Stern/Sloan Publishers, Inc.

POPEYE THE SAILOR and his three friends thought it was a perfect day for a picnic at sea. Olive Oyl packed a lunch. Swee'pea helped her, and Wimpy—well, Wimpy just hoped that there would be enough hamburgers for everybody, especially for himself.

While Wimpy rowed, and Olive trailed her hand in the water, Popeye told Swee'pea about his muscles. "This one," he pointed to a lump on his arm, "is for moving buildings, and this one," he pointed to his other arm, "is for moving mountains."

Swee'pea looked at his own teeny-weeny muscles. "If you eat your spinach every day, as I do," Popeye said, "you'll grow up to be as strong as I am." And he made an extra big muscle on both arms.

"Let's find an island and eat," Olive said, looking east. She saw nothing but water. Popeye looked south. He saw nothing but the sparkling sea. Wimpy turned his head and looked north. He saw nothing but little green waves. Swee'pea looked west and said, "Goo!" Sure enough, there was a black bump sticking out of the sea, just big enough for a picnic.

"There aren't any trees there," wailed Olive. But it seemed like a good place for a picnic and Wimpy headed the rowboat toward the little black island.

Popeye dropped the anchor overboard and they climbed out. Olive counted as Wimpy ate fourteen hamburgers. Popeye drank most of the soda pop. Swee'pea caught his finger in the pickle jar and Olive got it out, along with the last three pickles. When a drop of rain landed in Popeye's pipe, making it sizzle, they all agreed to leave. "Man the boat!" Popeye cried. But there was no boat!

Then something strange began to happen to the island. It was moving! First it wiggled and then it popped right out of the water. "Blow me down!" shouted Popeye. "This is no island. We're on a whale and we're floating out to sea!"

This whale was the roughest, toughest whale in the whole sea. When he woke from his nap to find picnickers on his back, he was simply furious. He tried to roll over. Olive caught Swee'pea, Wimpy rescued the lunch basket, and Popeye hung on to the whale's tail.

The whale rolled again. They all ran up one side and slid down the other. Then the whale bucked and turned and twisted and the waves grew higher and higher. Popeye and his friends were tossed about topsy-turvy.

"Do something, Popeye, do something!" Olive cried as she clung to Swee'pea. At once, Popeye knew what had to be done.

"Bring me my spinach!" he called. Olive whipped out a can of spinach, opened it and Popeye ate every bit. Then things really began to happen. Popeye's muscles grew like cabbages. He took the rope-line he carried on his belt and made a lariat. Twirling it round and round, like a cowboy, Popeye lassoed the whale about the jaws.

Olive and Swee'pea and Wimpy thought they were on a roller coaster as Popeye zoomed around the whale. In a short time he had his jaws tied so tightly that the whale became as gentle as a lamb. Then Olive spread the picnic blanket over the whale's back as if it were a saddle and Popeye rode him back toward shore.

On the way back, they caught up with their rowboat and Wimpy secured it to the whale's tail. Olive took one of the oars and tied a can of spinach to the end of it which she dangled in front of the whale. "It makes him go faster," she explained to everyone.

Everyone was on shore to greet them as they returned. The tugs tooted their horns. Of course, the whale was terribly embarrassed because no one was afraid of him any more. Even the little fishes were laughing at him.

Popeye gave all the credit to spinach. Then he said, "When you picnic on an island, be sure that it has trees on it. Then you can be sure it isn't a whale!"

Discover another delightful children's series
from Price/Stern/Sloan:

by Pamela Conn Beall and Susan Hagen Nipp

A collection of best-selling books and 60-minute cassettes
that children love!

WEE SING®
WEE SING® AND PLAY
WEE SING® SILLY SONGS
WEE SING® AROUND THE CAMPFIRE
WEE SING® FOR CHRISTMAS
WEE SING® NURSERY RHYMES AND LULLABIES
WEE SING® BIBLE SONGS

And activity-filled coloring books, cassettes and felt-tipped markers!

WEE COLOR® WEE SING
WEE COLOR® WEE SING AND PLAY
WEE COLOR® WEE SING SILLY SONGS
WEE COLOR® WEE SING AROUND THE CAMPFIRE
WEE COLOR® WEE SING FOR CHRISTMAS
WEE COLOR® WEE SING NURSERY RHYMES AND LULLABIES

The above P/S/S titles are available wherever books are sold,
or can be ordered directly from the publisher.

PRICE/STERN/SLOAN *Publishers, Inc.*
360 North La Cienega Boulevard, Los Angeles, California 90048